Gayle Black, BA,
Adelphi University
received a master's
administration from
Greenvale, New Yo
New York and has t
the Nassau County ~~~~~~~~~~~~~~~~~~ she has studied
nutrition and diet therapy for the past fourteen years,
both in Europe and the United States, and has served as
a consultant to physicians. She presently lives in New
York City, where she maintains a private practice.

Ms Black was assistant administrator of Bennet
Community Hospital, Fort Lauderdale, Florida, and
was elected US Representative in Health Care for one
year at St Thomas's Hospital, London, England; most
recently she held the position of assistant professor and
deputy chairperson of the Health Care Management
Department at St Francis College, Brooklyn,
New York.

She is a member of the American Public Health
Association, American Association of University
Professors, American Hospital Association of America,
Eta Sigma Phi Health Honor Society, the Royal Society
of Health and the American Federation of Astrologers.

The Sun Sign Diet
CAPRICORN
December 22–January 20

Gayle Black

Foreword by Ivan G. Black, M.D.

CORGI BOOKS

To the brightest stars in my universe . . .
my daughter, Margot, and my husband, Shelly . . .
whose love and encouragement kept me going.

THE SUN SIGN DIET
Capricorn: December 22–January 20

A CORGI BOOK 0 552 13149 0

First publication in Great Britain

PRINTING HISTORY
Macmillan Publishing Co. New York edition
published 1986
Corgi edition published 1987

NOTE on British Edition
The author does not accept any liability for any
alterations made to the original text. The publishers have
made every effort to find British equivalents in the diet
foods wherever possible.

This book is set in 10/11½ pt California
by Colset Private Limited, Singapore.

Corgi Books are published by Transworld Publishers
Ltd., 61–63 Uxbridge Road, Ealing, London W5 5SA, in
Australia by Transworld Publishers (Australia) Pty. Ltd.,
15–23 Helles Avenue, Moorebank, NSW 2170, and in
New Zealand by Transworld Publishers (N.Z.) Ltd.,
Cnr. Moselle and Waipareira Avenues, Henderson,
Auckland.

Made and printed in Great Britain by
Cox & Wyman Ltd., Reading, Berks.

Contents

Capricorn
December 22–January 20

FOREWORD

by Ivan G. Black, MD*

Gayle Black, the author of *The Sun Sign Diet*, has a fresh and simple answer to the question that is both the dieter's and the physician's major dilemma: if dieters are able to shed at least some unwanted pounds on a good diet, then why can't they manage to stay on the diet until they've lost the entire amount?

During my many years as a medical nutritionist, I have treated more than two thousand patients for the problem of obesity. It has been proven to me that there are many good diets, and that practically all of them have a chance of working if followed consistently. But for some heretofore mysterious reason, patients simply cannot hold to a diet for the time necessary to lose all the excess pounds.

Black gives us the reason. Diets designed with purely caloric or metabolic considerations in mind overlook several crucial elements: the dieter's particular temperament and particular personality traits – elements that have been part of the dieter's life from birth onwards. A diet designed for all people, or for an 'average' person, is doomed to failure from the start.

Like most doctors, I am familiar with the typical patterns of dieters. For the first few weeks they faithfully come to the office for their weekly visits. Usually there is an encouraging weight loss. Then, two or three weeks may pass without a visit. When the patients finally do return, they sheepishly tell of feeling too guilty and embarrassed to come in for the checkup and weigh-in

Dr Black is no relation to the author.

because they broke the diet and regained some or all of the initial weight lost.

I have seen how various patients respond differently to my advice. Some patients demand that I yell at them like a drill sergeant when they do not achieve a good weight loss. It helps them do better the next week. Other patients want me to treat them as a kind and gentle grandfather would treat a beloved grandchild. This, I must state, is really asking a doctor to play God. How does one figure out how individual dieters prefer to be handled? Gayle Black eloquently and comprehensively communicates the diversity in individuals and delivers the proper approach for each dieter.

My experience in private practice has convinced me that some people do much better on simple repetitive diets, while others fail if they do not have variety in their prescribed dieting plan. Because *The Sun Sign Diet* addresses the needs peculiar to the individual, and allows for those occasional 'bad days', the reducing diets presented here work! And they work without the dieter feeling deprived or frustrated . . . or guilty!

Besides being a nutritional doctor, I am also a sports medicine physician and have treated countless athletes for a myriad of injuries. Often, an athlete who is in superb condition will set a record one week, while the following week, under identical circumstances and for no apparent reason, he will perform way below the previous week's level.

Similarly, I have patients who lose five pounds one week, then eat the exact same food the following week and lose no weight at all. I have also noticed weeks when none of my patients has a good loss, as well as other weeks when everyone seems to be losing. I have found that there are certain days when many of my patients show an almost uniform twenty-point rise above their normal blood pressure, while on other days there may be a twenty-point drop.

With no clinical or pathological reasons to account for these phenomena, it was at this point that I acknowledged that there seemed to be a definite relationship between atmospheric conditions and the functioning of the human body. And I have seen many illnesses, from rheumatism to allergies, react to climate and season changes. Certainly, in my professional practice, I have noticed how the healing process is affected by changes in climatic conditions. And I have also noticed that at particular times of the year I hear from old patients who desire to start a diet again. Once again, supposedly inexplicable patterns emerge.

In addition to offering explanations for these atmospheric and climatic phenomena, *The Sun Sign Diet* offers detailed individual personality profiles and guidelines on individual eating habits. These can be a valuable aid to both patient and doctor.

Diets work, and they will work for a lifetime, if they take into consideration every aspect of a person's lifestyle. Rather than focusing merely on the effects of overeating, Gayle Black concentrates on the physical and emotional needs of individual dieters. I heartily applaud her for considering the whole person and whole lifestyle in her approach and in the preparation of these diets. *The Sun Sign Diet* provides nutritionally balanced foods with a high percentage of essential vitamins, minerals, carbohydrates, proteins, fats, and fibre.

I was delighted to support Gayle Black and to allow her to work with my patients, who filled out lengthy questionnaires as part of the documentation for her exhaustive research. I heartily recommend that dieters use the valuable information contained in *The Sun Sign Diet* to assist them in achieving successful weight reduction and in finding a lifetime maintenance programme.

New York City   IVAN G. BLACK, MD
1 February 1986

PREFACE

Astrology is all about balance — balance on a cosmic scale. The astrologer attempts to bring you into balance with the changing universe. Astrology is, perhaps, the most natural of the sciences. It holds that nature, in spite of its excesses and mysteries, is, ultimately, order. The nature of the changing universe affects our lives. What happens up there has something to do with what happens down here.

Cause and effect.

I was lucky. I was born under a star that guaranteed that I would find my way to astrology and health care. 'Lucky', in this case, is a relative term.

In 1958, I almost died.

It was just after my sixteenth birthday when I came down with Guillain-Barré Syndrome. You probably have never heard of it, and I pray you never get this vicious virus. It attacks the nervous system, the musculature, and the reflexes. In my case, it affected my eyes, and I could not see for months. After spending nine months in the hospital, the prognosis was still grim. My doctors did not believe I could ever regain control over my weak body.

They were wrong.

Fortunately more than one valid medical system has been created under the sun.

In the East, astrology is often an integral part of the diagnostic and healing process. Although our Western medical technology can help raise the standard of living and improve health care in the East, we should not discard ancient truths, truths that have survived and, indeed, flourished up until this day. We have a lot to learn from each other.

Balance.

When you come as close to the edge as I did, lying in that hospital bed, profound thoughts run through your mind. Modern medicine was doing as much as it could for me. But I knew there just had to be something else.

Yoga.

The year was 1959, and the yoga centre my family brought me to was on the top floor of a seedy office building in some obscure section of New York City. The setting was bleak. There was a candle and a mat on the floor. But there was also the illuminating aura of a beautiful swami. He claimed that even though this horrible Guillain-Barré Syndrome had worked over my body pretty thoroughly, he could restore my health.

He was right.

But it wasn't easy. I threw myself into this ancient system and worked harder than I ever imagined I could. The stakes were high, but I had motivation: I was trying to regain control over my body, over my life.

And six months later I did.

An illness led me to yoga, and yoga would eventually lead me to astrology. It was a perfectly natural progression.

Cause and effect.

I became a yoga zealot. I had a mission. I wanted to tell the world about it: I wanted to repay this ancient system for giving me back my life. So I studied. I studied intensively for ten years, asked questions, and studied even more, until I became a certified yoga instructor.

My mind was transforming as well. So, while I continued my spiritual studies, I also worked towards a degree in psychology at Adelphi University. Armed with my credentials, I thought I had a lot of the answers.

But I still had a lot to learn.

14

I met another swami, who told me that if I was really serious about yoga and healing, I had to fill a void in my spiritual education; I had to learn astrology. And if I was ever to become a truly effective health-care provider, I had to move to an even higher level and study medical astrology.

From the moment we are born, our bodies and personalities are affected by the position of the sun. This influence will continue throughout our lifetimes. It may all be quite simple, but I have to admit that I'm still amazed by it, especially when I find myself accurately determining the lifestyle of a person just by referring to his or her natal chart.

When I was invited by the British government to share notes with some of their health-care professionals, at the prestigious St Thomas's Hospital in London, I rubbed elbows with doctors from every corner of the globe. I met doctors from India who not only had studied yoga, philosophy, and Eastern culture but who also had trained at the finest medical schools in India. A great number of them, in fact many of the people I met there, were extremely knowledgeable about astrology. Many spoke of its great potential for unlocking medical mysteries.

My spiritual awareness paralleled my academic development. Not only was I in an environment that gave astrology its due, but, in my capacity as observer, I was able to see firsthand how powerful the stars really are. There are no accidents.

I spent a good deal of time with the patients at St Thomas's. Examining their charts, the first thing I did was carefully note each patient's date of birth. Then, based on the patient's sun sign and transiting planets, I found that in most cases I could pick out obvious maladies or medical problems before even seeing them.

The hospital was my laboratory, and I became a researcher. I probed, I prodded, I questioned everyone and everything. I couldn't have been in a better place, with access to patients' histories and all the medical minds around me.

It all began to make sense. I kept clear and concise notes.

Why do we have periodic bouts with illness? Why do we have cyclical episodes at seven- and/or fourteen-year intervals?

Surgical patients provided revelation after revelation. I noted that if surgery was performed during a Mercury retrograde, the patient usually had to go back for more repair and further surgery. Years later, when I told a dear friend to delay stomach surgery for three weeks, she asked me why. When I told her that Mercury was in retrograde, she did what any rational person would do: she told me that I was crazy and that the surgeon, rather than the stars, had set the date for the operation. That was one time when I hated to be right, but three months later she was back under the knife.

In medical astrology, the sun has rulership over different parts of the body. And I observed that Jupiter's position affected blood chemistry, usually showing up as diabetes and/or low blood sugar.

I also discovered the role the seasons played. Summer claimed higher birth weights, with June and July the top months. The preponderance of births occurred in June: the mortality rate was always higher in winter.

And, I wondered, was it a coincidence that many patients died at almost the same hour of the day that they were born?

Balance?

England also introduced me to the practice of homeopathy. The use of herbs and cell salts to treat certain diseases and conditions is an ancient and revered science in Europe. Thousands of years ago, the ancients discovered that there was a correlation between the herbs and cell salts, the disease, and the position of those planets whose course a doctor could follow.

Losing weight had always been a constant problem for me. Like so many people, I had spent years getting acquainted with diet doctors, clinics, and amphetamines. Struggling, gaining, losing, succeeding – but ultimately failing. I lived for next week's diet encounter group. I tried everything.

Then something quite profound occurred to me.

I reasoned that if sun signs had so much power over health and well-being, why couldn't that power be harnessed to help one lose weight? And maintain weight?

So I decided to design my own diet. A diet based on the vitamins, minerals, nutrients, cell salts, and all the properties governed by my sun sign. A diet that would, hopefully, balance my system, that would, by the very foods I consumed, eliminate my constant battle of the bulge.

And it worked.

For the past several years I have been using the sun sign diet for my private clients, and, due to the success I've had with hundreds of people, I've gained a reputation as a weight loss guru. But I'm not a magician, nor do I possess any supernatural powers. I can claim only a small part of the credit for my clients' success. After all, the stars impel – they do not compel. I have succeeded because I talk directly to people and address their special needs.

When I tell my Aries clients that they eat on the run, grabbing food on the way out of the door, they are amazed at how much I know about them. When I tell Cancers that I understand their insatiable craving for sweets, and that it is not in their heads, they know that I am talking directly to them. And when I sympathize with the Virgos' picky eating habits and dislike of food additives, they are relieved to be talking to someone who really knows them.

Everybody is different. We each have to travel our own path to transformation. With this insight, a healthy,

17

trimmer body is within everyone's reach.

Listen to your body. It not only knows what it wants, but it naturally wants what it needs.

Balance.

ACKNOWLEDGEMENTS

I want to express my thanks to my creative Libra agent, Mel Berger of the William Morris Agency, whose enthusiasm, encouragement, and energy made the publication of this book possible.

To Hillel Black, a dynamic, positive Aries, and Arlene Friedman, a progressive, insightful Taurus, of the Macmillan Publishing Company, who first recognized the value of this work and its potential for helping individuals finally win the personal weight battle.

To my very special Gemini friend, Jill Cooper, whose extraordinary help, love, and talent guided me, and whose friendship sustained me.

To Marian Cohn, another creative, talented Libra whose professional expertise assisted me in the preparation of this book.

To Robert Schaefer, who got me off to a flying start, and to Rachel Rothschild, Gill Ziff, Betty Rothbardt, Eileen Kurtis-Kleinman, Seymour Feig, Jane Dakin, Michael Cole, Diane Powers, Jackie Seplow, Dorothy and Morton Pavane, Florine Dorfmann, and Dr Constance Buxer, who were always there when I needed them.

To Joyce and Nick Monte, Keepers of the International Health and Beauty Spa at Gurney's Inn, Montauk, New York, who supported me in my research and allowed me to conduct hundreds of interviews with their approving guests. And similarly, to Frieda Eisenkraft, director and owner of the lovely Deerfield Manor, East Stroudsburg, Pennsylvania, who graciously opened her spa to my research.

To all my friends, who understood my commitment to this project and who left me alone. To my clients, who waited so patiently for their appointments and who accepted the many cancellations. And to the thousands of wonderful people from continent to continent, who took the time and had the patience to fill out my lengthy questionnaires.

My heartfelt gratitude and appreciation to you all.

PUBLISHER'S NOTE ON BRITISH EDITION

Should any of the foods mentioned in *The Sun Sign Diet* be unavailable or difficult to purchase in the UK, readers will probably not find it hard — by using a little imagination and common sense — to choose a suitable alternative as an equivalent in calorific and nutritional values.

UK equivalents for US measures

An American pint = 16 fluid oz
An English pint = 20 fluid oz
An American cup measure = 8 fluid oz
All American spoon measures are a flat spoonful
An American tablespoon = 3 flat teaspoons

INTRODUCTION

If you want to lose 3 to 5 pounds a week, eat many of the foods you crave, binge on sinful foods four times a month, and dine in the most elegant gourmet restaurants, this diet is for you. The Sun Sign Diet has worked for thousands of people and is a revolutionary approach to dieting. The Sun Sign Diet helps you explore and understand how your own sexuality relates to overeating. It helps you recognize and change self-sabotaging habits. You will learn which food combinations best meet your personal weight loss goals. Whether at home, on the job, or dining with friends or business associates, the Sun Sign Diet helps you achieve your ideal weight without ever feeling hungry. You will learn the secrets to lifetime thinness.

Medical science has ascertained that everyone's chemical, mineral and vitamin needs are different — and yet diets are prepared for the masses. But you and your body chemistry are not general; you're unique. For a diet to work you must take into consideration your own specific needs. One of the wonder diets may work for you . . . another may not. If a diet does not meet your individual needs, it's ultimately destined to fail.

We each have our own astrological blueprint, a stamp of our special identity. A natal horoscope indicates to all individuals the weakest and strongest parts of their bodies. Certain health problems are peculiar to each zodiac sign. Have you ever noticed how some months you are more irritable or depressed, or totally incapable of following a diet? This can be attributed in part to the fact that we are all influenced by the rotation of the planets.

The sun is the most powerful force in the heavens: the controller of human vitality. Scientists who have studied its light report that all elements on earth are represented in solar radiation. It should come as no surprise then that the sun signs are extremely significant in astrology; 75 per cent of the time the sun sign will reign supreme over all the other planets in one's birth chart.

Over the years I have found that, invariably, people's behaviour, desire, motivations and habits fall into the twelve zodiac signs: Aries, Taurus, Gemini, and so on. Each sign bestows upon you mental and emotional characteristics, even an individual body type and structure, and specific psychological proclivities.

Human bodies come in twelve different shapes, represented by the twelve signs. Research has indicated that people of the same zodiac sign have a basic genetic form and a tendency to develop fat in the same localized areas. By recognizing the conscious and unconscious components of your psyche, you will be able to avoid the dieting pitfalls that have plagued you up to now. By studying those conscious and unconscious factors and understanding their importance in the dieting process, you can gain control of your eating for the first time. You will no longer be ruled by impulsive or compulsive eating. You will be in control.

Obviously, you have never found the ideal weight loss programme. Most diets are not planned for individual likes, dislikes, cravings, and predetermined fondness for food.

With this diet you never have to fail again.

By combining a nutritionally sound approach to dieting, taking into consideration ancient therapies and modern medicine, I have designed a programme that incorporates behavioural characteristics, personality traits, libidinal tendencies, and chemical and metabolic makeup. Now anyone, at any age, can maintain a healthy body weight and can expect to add years to their life, in addition to finally conquering their overweight.

Under your special sun sign, I describe your personality profile and eating habits, along with inherent behaviour patterns that often spell success or failure in the dieting process. You will readily recognize yourself. (If you are on the 'cusp', read the cusp section *in addition to your sun sign*.)

The reducing diets are designed to produce an average weight loss of 3 to 5 pounds per week. Included in each reducing diet is a list of supplemental vitamins and minerals which are vital to your well-being. Some of the reducing diets offer you choices in the foods you consume; others do not allow for any substitutions. You will note that each sun sign diet has carefully planned, specifically tailored reducing diets, some programmed for more than two weeks and some for as little as three days. A diet is only successful when the motivations, behavioural patterns and nutritional demands of each individual are considered, and these diets have been designed for your lifestyle and temperament and should not be interchanged with diets of other signs.

There are no transgressions when you follow The Sun Sign Diet. It is biochemically created to replenish your body with necessary cell salts, nutrients and fuel for optimum daily functioning.

Forget what you've experienced on all other diets: on the Sun Sign Diet, you will lose weight and feel more alive than you ever have before in your life. The sun sign diet takes the total person approach and considers your total lifestyle.

I have included a lifetime maintenance food list, from which you will have the option to choose your own menus. To get started, included are two sample maintenance menus and instructions on handling maintenance planning, special-occasion dining, restaurant eating and food shopping.

In fact, you don't even have to think of it as a diet. Instead, consider it a way of life. You will not have to subject yourself to any guilt for the inevitable cheating that can occur. Last, but not least, your diet takes into consideration the fact that you are human. And being human you have certain sensory cravings. On this diet, you will be allowed to eat many of the foods you crave. I have even included a binge day for each of you, permitting the foods which give you that ultimate sense of satisfaction – the foods you crave.

How do I know what foods you crave?

It is written in the stars, and follow the stars to the last diet you will ever need.

YOUR SUN SIGN

The stars determine the way you eat.

Aries	March 21 – April 20	the hit-and-run eater
Taurus	April 21 – May 21	the gourmet eater
Gemini	May 22 – June 21	the erratic eater
Cancer	June 22 – July 23	the emotional eater
Leo	July 24 – August 23	the restaurant eater
Virgo	August 24 – September 23	the analytical eater
Libra	September 24 – October 23	the balanced eater
Scorpio	October 24 – November 22	the sensuous eater
Sagittarius	November 23 – December 21	the optimistic eater
Capricorn	December 22 – January 20	the disciplined eater
Aquarius	January 21 – February 19	the experimental eater
Pisces	February 20 – March 20	the ambivalent eater

General Diet and Maintenance Guidelines for All Sun Signs

THE IMPORTANCE OF DRINKING WATER

To lose weight, you must drink eight glasses of water each day.

WHAT FUNCTION DOES WATER PLAY IN YOUR BODY?

- Aids in chemical changes that take place in the body.
- Carries food to and wastes away from the body's cells.
- As urine, flushes away wastes of metabolism. Wastes increase during weight reduction, since fat is being broken down for energy.
- Used in digestion as saliva (about one gallon per day) and in digestive enzymes (about one-half gallon per day).
- Regulates your temperature by insulation or evaporation of perspiration.
- Maintains muscle tone. If you do not consume enough water, your muscles will eventually become soft and flabby.

HOW CAN YOU FIGHT FLUID RETENTION?

The most important way is by drinking more water. This will produce more sodium excretion. *Drinking more water will actually prevent the body from storing it,* which the body does when insufficient amounts are taken in. This is a survival reaction of the body, since every necessary chemical reaction must occur in body fluid.

HOW DOES INADEQUATE WATER INTAKE CONTRIBUTE TO OBESITY?

Your kidneys need water to filter the toxic wastes of normal metabolism. Without an adequate amount of water, the body produces less urine. For further self-preservation, the body then uses the liver to detoxify the blood. However, then one of the other functions of the liver — fat and carbohydrate metabolism — is neglected. This causes fat to be dumped into storage areas instead of being used for energy, and obviously results in further obesity.

WHY IS WATER STRESSED IN PREFERENCE TO OTHER FLUIDS?

- Water, especially bottled water, has very few impurities.
- Most fizzy drinks have sodium (or salt additives) as a preservative, which, we know, is a cause of fluid retention.
- Fizzy drinks get us hooked on sugar, and we then start craving other sweets.
- Coffee and tea are not as good as water due to their caffeine content, which stimulates the appetite.

Remember: all sun signs must follow water advice, all signs need water, so start drinking it now.

- You may healthfully repeat this diet until your desired weight is achieved.
- Drink low-calorie drinks to insure better weight loss.
- Many times you will not find a beverage indicated after a meal in your own reducing diet. If not

specifically listed, you may choose from the beverage list, noted in your 'General Guidelines'.

- You will note that I often do not include coffee with milk. Do not add milk to your coffee if not indicated; it will upset the enzyme action and you will not lose weight. Try to get used to drinking your coffee black, or switch to tea. Occasionally, when there is no fruit in your reducing diet meal, you may, if you absolutely must, have 2 oz of milk in your coffee. Just remember, it will slow down your weight loss.
- Remember, you must drink 8 glasses of water each day, regardless of any other liquid you consume.
- Choose your condiments from the seasonings list.
- Consider the most likely times during the month that you are under stress emotionally or physically; plan for the 'binge days' with that in mind. Women should consider their unique cravings during and before their menstrual cycle.
- Read all the notes, and your diet regime before going to sleep each night, for education, motivation and information.
- Awake with a positive approach, knowing that you are on your way to a heavenly body.
- At the conclusion of your individual Sun Sign Diet, carefully read 'Maintaining Your Ideal Weight' for lifelong success and fitness.

SHOPPING LIST OF SEASONINGS, EXTRACTS, AND DIET AIDS

BEVERAGES

Black coffee (regular and decaffeinated)
Tea
Herbal teas
Iced tea sweetened with calorie-free sweetener
Low-calorie sparkling drinks (without salt additives)
Mineral water
Perrier
Remember: all carbonated drinks contain additives that make for the carbonation. It is far better and will insure better weight if you drink just plain water.

CONDIMENTS

Apple cider vinegar
Bouillon cubes
Diet jelly
Low-cholesterol margarine
Gelatin in unsweetened fruit juice for low-calorie jelly
(For diabetics) Jelly available from Boots the Chemist
Bovril cube dissolved in water
Horseradish
Lemon juice (concentrate or fresh)
Low-calorie soups
No-oil salad dressing (or substitute other 2 calorie salad dressing)*
Sugar substitute (Sweet 'n Low)
* No-oil salad dressing can be prepared with lemon juice or wine vinegar, and salt, pepper and mustard.

HERBS AND SPICES

Basil
Cayenne pepper
Chervil
Chives
Cinnamon
Curry powder
Dill
Garlic
Ginger
Kelp
Marjoram
Oregano
Parsley
Pepper
Peppercorns
Peppermint
Sage
Thyme

DIET AIDS

Glucomannan (or an equivalent form of dietary fibre) — 2 capsules a half hour before meals, total six capsules daily. And remember: 8 glasses of water a day.
* Note: these items are allowed only while on maintenance eating, unless indicated specifically on your diet.

MAINTENANCE EATING HINTS

Being fat is not an accident; it is a lifestyle. To lose weight permanently and to keep it off, a diet must fit your lifestyle, make you feel good, give you energy, and allow you to exist on this planet without feeling deprived.

You will note in your individual sun sign chapter that I have listed special maintenance foods. These foods are governed by your sun sign, and I suggest that you choose as many foods as possible from that list. I also include a 2,000-calorie sample maintenance diet for your individual sun sign, and I suggest that you use your own creativity to design your own maintenance menus. But first you will need to determine the number of calories per day needed for maintenance, based on the following, generally accepted equations for measuring the calorie-to-weight ratio. Multiply your *ideal* weight by:

- 13, if sedentary;
- 15, if moderately active;
- 20, if vigorously strenuous.

Example
Ideal weight 120 pounds, sedentary = 1,560 calories/day.

Purchase a good calorie book. For those of you who will be counting carbohydrates, you will have to test out your maintenance carbo level, which is usually about 100 grams.

After you have reached your goal weight, weigh yourself every three or four days. If you have gained 3 pounds, resume your diet regimen with any day of your sun sign reducing diet. If you have gained more than 5 pounds, begin again with Day One of your sun sign reducing diet.

How can you allow for bingeing while on maintenance eating? If you allow yourself a daily calorie count of 1,500 calories, programme it for the week (i.e. 1,500 calories × 7 = 10,500 calories per week). If you know that you want to splurge for a certain meal, be sure to deduct the calorie count of that meal from the total weekly calorie allowance. In this way you can adjust your eating over the entire week and you will not have that starved feeling. NOTE: Never plan less than 1,000 maintenance calories per day.

Is it harder for some people to lose weight than it is others? Yes. There are many differences in metabolism, often influenced by an individual's sun sign. That is why, for the very first time, you will succeed on this diet where other diets have failed. Each reducing diet is designed to address the chemical makeup and uniqueness of your sun sign.

RESTAURANT EATING TIPS

Your boss asks you to entertain a client at one of the finer Italian restaurants in town, or your girlfriends plan a baby shower at a quaint French restaurant. For many dieters, eating out is their downfall on an otherwise successful diet. Observe the following guidelines and you will not have to worry about enjoying the pleasures of a good restaurant meal.

GENERAL RESTAURANT EATING GUIDELINES

- Always order water the moment you sit down. Order a pitcher of water and start drinking. Have at least two glasses.
- If you wish to order wine, you may. If you choose not to, order coffee or tea when others order their

alcoholic beverages. Don't worry, they will not think you are strange. Many people do this, and the caffeine in the tea or coffee will give you a lift. If you wish to limit your caffeine intake, order mineral water or fruit juice. NOTE: This is all done to keep you away from the rolls or garlic bread.

- Ask that dressing not be added to your salad. You may always use lemon and/or vinegar.
- Request whatever you want prepared the way you want it. Don't accept fried when broiled or steamed is your desire. Don't be embarrassed. You are there to be served.
- Remember, the smaller the portion, the more you'll lose.

Your individual sun sign chapter includes restaurant eating menus that reflect the foods you like. Follow the suggestions in 'Restaurant Eating' in your sun sign section, as well as those that appear below, and you will enjoy dining out without jeopardizing your successful dieting and maintenance eating.

DO'S AND DON'TS

CHINESE RESTAURANTS

- Do not allow the chef to use MSG (monosodium glutamate) in your food.
- Do not order anything prepared with cornstarch.
- Do not order anything fried in batter.
- Do order anything poached, steamed, stir-fried, or simmered in natural juices.
- Do drink lots of tea.
- Do order white rice.

ITALIAN RESTAURANTS

- Do not order heavy cheese sauces or dishes.
- Do not order anything swimming in oil or butter.
- Do not order fried food.
- Do order food in a light tomato sauce, or prepared with garlic and/or wine.
- Do eat a small portion of pasta.
  NOTE: When ordering pasta, order only linguine, capellini, or fettucine.

AMERICAN RESTAURANTS

- Do not order casseroles (they are filled with all sorts of no-no's).
- Do not order food breaded and fried.
- Do not order food prepared with mayonnaise.

JAPANESE RESTAURANTS

- Do not order anything fried.

ALL ABOUT 'CUSP PERIODS'

If your birthday falls during one of the cusp periods listed below, you will have planetary influences from two signs, or as we say in astrology, you are 'on the cusp' of two signs.

> Sagittarius and Capricorn
> December 19–23
>
> Capricorn and Aquarius
> January 19–22

Since your eating behaviour will be influenced by the influence of the cusp period, you will want to read about this special period *in addition* to reading your sun sign chapter. Most people are familiar with their zodiac sun sign, but even those people born on the cusp are often unacquainted with what that means. According to traditional astrology, the cusp is the twenty-four-hour period in which the planets in the solar system move into a new position in the zodiac; thus you are receiving influences from the new ruling sun sign as well as some influences from the old. For example, on January 21 the zodiac sun sign moves from Capricorn to Aquarius. That day is called the 'cusp of Capricorn – Aquarius', and while anyone born on that day is a Capricorn, many Aquarius traits will be evident in personality and eating habits.

Many astrologers, myself included, believe that cusp influences are evident not only in individuals born on the exact day of the cusp, but also in anyone born during the few days of the *cusp period*. My observations of the food personalities of these people indicate that the cusp period actually seems to begin about two to three days before the end of one sun sign and to extend two days into the beginning of the next.

What does this mean to you, practically speaking? If you were born during the first two days of one sun sign *or* the last two or three days of the next, your personality will display a blend of traits from both signs on your cusp, and I would suggest that you read the personality profiles for both sun signs in the relevant book in this series to get a complete picture of your own food personality.

However, although your birthday falls in the 'cusp period', *you only have claim to one sun sign, as shown in 'Your Sun Sign' at the beginning of the book*. The sun is by far the largest member of the solar system – about 740 times more massive than its nine major planets combined, and ten times wider than the largest planet, Jupiter. The sun's rays are the strongest in the solar system, and therefore, your sun sign (as determined by the position of the sun in relation to the earth on the day you were born) *always* rules about 80 per cent of your health, behaviour, and nutritional and chemical makeup. It is for this reason that you must follow the diet and nutrition plans designed specifically for your sun sign.

SAGITTARIUS – CAPRICORN

You have more control over your diet than your Sagittarian friends seem to have, so consider yourself fortunate at having been born on this cusp. The carefree attitude of Sagittarius has been tempered by the ever-driving, goal-oriented Capricorn tenacity, and you will feel guilty when you cheat. That's Capricorn telling you that you will never walk the path to success that way. So you are caught between hoping your diet problem will take care of itself, and really knowing that nothing will change if you are not the master of your eating destiny. With regard to dieting, you often take a light view of a weighty subject.

CAPRICORN – AQUARIUS

This can be a most beneficial cusp. The Capricorn part of you is 'determined' to lose weight and will persevere, and the Aquarius part of you is often too involved with work and projects to think about food. In addition, you are one cusp that is usually 'nutritionally savvy' and can accomplish anything you set your mind to do (even if it means eating with chopsticks).

A WORD OF ADVICE

When reading about the behaviour patterns of your unique sun sign, there may be statements with which you disagree. Please keep in mind the following: often, many of our true (subconscious) feelings never surface. Allow yourself to be free and open, and understand that not all desires and tendencies are – for many individual reasons – manifested on a conscious level.

The Capricorn Personality

'He that is master of himself will soon be master of others.'

I f you are aware of and emphasize the positive personality traits with which you were born, this diet will work for you. You, Capricorn, are most of the time an excellent dieter, because there is a part of you that handles the rigours of self-denial quite well. You have a healthy respect for self-control. You are very disciplined, goal oriented, well-organized, have great determination

41

and tremendous inner strength. You love and need a challenge. What a powerhouse of fine qualities to bring to this diet.

To the above you can add great willpower, tenacity, and perseverance; and you are very good at adhering to details. You are a cautious person. You consider yourself the master of your own destiny, and will search to find the perfect solution to everything. Not surprisingly, you usually do find it. Your strong convictions and your ability to overcome almost all obstacles certainly say, 'Okay. I am ready to start dieting and I won't allow myself or anyone else to sabotage my plans.'

Now that you are feeling pretty good about yourself, I know that you will take your dieting commitment seriously. You take all commitments seriously. You are not afraid to put in the effort it takes to stick with a diet because you believe that you get what you work for. You set lofty goals and you reach them. No matter how long you have to pursue something, the knowledge that you will ultimately succeed keeps you right on course. You are truly the sign that understands the adage, 'knowledge is power'.

One of the major causes of illness for Capricorn is your tendency to bottle up emotions – in fact, you sometimes give the impression of not having any. Capricorns will carefully conceal pain so no one knows you are suffering. Your innate sense of dignity and propriety inhibits you from expressing your innermost feelings. You like to keep a low profile and you really don't feel comfortable being with people who go overboard expressing their emotions. You have a tendency to be shy and, perhaps, more serious than your friends. You must work to develop a sense of compassion for your own weaknesses and those of others. And, most importantly Capricorn, you must learn to release your tensions, both physically and verbally.

Your career is one of the most important things in your

42

life. You have a tendency to be a workaholic, and often expect other people to have the same ability and tendency. You are a hard taskmaster but never ask anyone to do something you would not do yourself. If you don't allow enough time to do a job perfectly, you'll come up with the perfect exuse – 'But I didn't have enough time.' The Capricorn personality does not thrive being pushed or threatened. You will respond to reason and a sense of duty. The best way to approach you is to appeal to your need to be needed.

You like to follow tried and true methods and often reflect on the past. You have an excellent memory for days gone by and remember the smallest details of events that happened long ago. You use life's experiences, rather than intuition, as guidelines for most decision making. But destiny somehow has a way of piling up the pounds, and though Capricorn is usually moderate in eating and drinking, even the most controlled Capricorn will at one point need to diet. However, that is a fact that you will not share with anyone. You will just diet – and won't talk about it. You are hypersensitive about weight gain because you feel it is a sign of weakness and loss of control. And to lose control is intolerable to you.

Capricorns are perfectionists and also demand perfection in their body. Your body represents a strong and firm foundation and you intend to take care of it for the rest of your life. This gives you a deep concern for the foods you consume and this is why you are probably opposed to eating foods with additives and preservatives.

Capricorns worry. You worry about your business, your family, your health, yesterday's news and tomorrow's IRS audit. You worry about social security and your pension plan, even if you are not due to collect it for twenty years. Under pressure you might throw caution to the wind. When your life becomes emotionally stressing, you become irritable, depressed, detached. At this point, if you decide to binge, it will be with ice cream, creamy

43

pies, cakes, breads, and traditional foods like Mum used to make. You were born with a wisdom beyond your years, however, and you old goats are much too responsible and self-controlled to indulge very long in a devil-may-care diet.

SEXUAL APPETITE

You are a tiger or tigress in the boardroom, but you are somewhat timid and modest in the bedroom. Capricorns are in need of a great deal of touching, holding, loving, and sex. And while you are not the most demonstrative sign of the zodiac, on a one-to-one basis you are quite smouldering, sexy Capricorn, capable of great sexual endurance. You Capricorns need to learn to show more of your sexual vulnerability. You need a little dose of immoral courage. And you need proof. You will devise little tests to prove that love is real. When you commit to a sexual relationship it must provide protection and security.

When the sexual revolution arrived along with the women's movement, for the first time it seemed possible that women could receive the same sexual gratification as men with no strings attached. Capricorn women discovered lust and passion, and it was an important discovery; however, lust and passion only with nice men. Sometimes, Capricorn, you are torn between the right kind of person and the person who turns you on. Many a Capricorn has gained weight pondering this difficult choice.

Letting go sexually involves an opening up – both physically and emotionally. And that sort of opening up involves trust. It means saying, 'I'm going to feel whatever I feel at a given moment. If I feel passionate, I'm not going to hold myself back.' The ability to let go is no small task for you. However, once you do you will emerge, radiant and in touch with your sexuality.

Usually, Capricorn, you have a lot of patience with your mate because you are willing to struggle like a mountain goat to reach the top of the mountain. David Viscott, noted psychologist, must have had Capricorns in mind when he said:

Relationships seldom die because they suddenly have no life left in them. They wither slowly, either because people do not understand how much or what kind of upkeep, time, work, love and caring they require or because people are too lazy or afraid to try. A relationship is a living thing. It needs and benefits from the same attention to detail that an artist lavishes on his art.

You Capricorns are extremely loyal sexual partners and demand the same loyalty from your mate. When sex is not readily available, or if you have been turned down by your partner, you may confuse sexual hunger with physical hunger. You go right to the refrigerator. And what do you eat? Bread, ice cream, or some other sweet. While satisfying your sweet tooth will temporarily make up for the feeling of rejection, you will pay for it in excess pounds in the long run.

If you become more aware of and learn to monitor this problem, you will find that you have a better handle on some of the subconscious patterns that make you eat for the sexually lean times. Plan ahead. Have other options readily available: read a good book, exercise, jump rope, jog.

Most important, you must communicate your needs to your partner. Often, dear Capricorn, the problem is that you cannot or do not ask for sex as often as you would like it. That's your homework assignment; it will help keep you skinny.

EATING/ENTERTAINING AT HOME

The Capricorn home says 'welcome'. It bespeaks your love of comfort, earthiness, and tradition, and in it your dinner guests will always find a pleasant refuge. You eschew the decorate look for the personal touch, and whether your style is strictly of a period or passionately eclectic the effect will be undeniably soft and cushiony. Your furnishings tend to be classic, understated, accented by beautiful artifacts, oriental rugs, quality wood tables, unusual collectibles. Your own handicrafts are likely to be on display, probably near your favourite spot in the house, your woodburning fireplace.

For you, entertaining at home is an opportunity to share the love, life, and friendship of your guests. You have the ability to throw a dinner party worthy of the award of excellence and still provide your company with a sense they are partaking in a simple, satisfying home-cooked meal. A damask tablecloth sets the stage of your formal dining room table, adorned with sterling silverware, individualized crystal salt and pepper shakers, fresh-cut flowers, and your favourite limited-edition china. (You are the type to turn over a plate just to make note of its origin.) You are thoroughbreds and entertain with an innate touch of class. You take great pains to organize the seating arrangements, and are very conscious of the likes and dislikes of your guests. (You are likely to keep such information catalogued, along with your recipes, on your home computer.) You love on such occasions to bring out your favourite vintage wine from your cabinet and present it to your guests with an introductory speech about its heritage that would impress the toughest critic.

As for the meal, you will choose from a repertoire of dishes based on award-winning recipes from *Good Housekeeping*, from your mother's favourite specialities, or from traditional holiday menus. You maintain a well-organized recipe box which enables you to adapt your meals to anyone's tastes without requiring extraordinary expense, and your butcher block kitchen is designed for your practical methods of cooking.

Many of your childhood memories are intertwined with the aromas and flavours of long-ago meals. And you enjoy preparing hot chocolate or hearty franks and sauerkraut for your own family and friends because you feel you are enriching their own future memories of their time with you. You are definitely a family-oriented person who is quite traditional. Thanksgiving, Christmas, Passover – holiday celebrations with all the customary trimmings – are always celebrated in your home. Lots of Capricorns own pianos because you associate the solid massiveness of this instrument with stability, permanence, security. Besides, nothing pleases you more than to have your company sing along with some nostalgic tunes. You almost feel that it is your responsibility as a mother, father, daughter, son . . . or *Capricorn*, to make these holidays festive.

With food so symbolic of sentiment and love, you must work extra hard to stay with a diet, Capricorn. You often say to yourself, how can I resist joining my loved ones for a midnight snack? Well, just think about how often you have soothed your harried nerves with a tall glass of milk and a generous hunk of chocolate cake only to regret the calories later, and I know you realistic Capricorns will find the inner resolve to forego any future late-night parties around the kitchen table.

When all is said and done, you usually do not like fancy preparations if you are not entertaining, despite your superb culinary skills and the fact that it warms your heart to feed a friend. You consider it a waste of time to spend your life cooking and cleaning when there are more important things to be done – like working.

Before you go food shopping you are sure to check to see what food items need to be replaced. No double guessing, for you, Capricorn. You have a sophisticated (practically computerized) system for filing coupons. You have even thought about marketing your own food shopping programme. You often write your list according to the arrangement of the supermarket; or at the very least you have grouped items into categories, such as 'dairy', 'household', 'frozen foods'. This precision almost always guarantees that you will arrive home without forgotten purchases.

Because you often worry about the future and the unknown, you tend to plan ahead when it comes to buying groceries. You have enough food supplies tucked away in your cupboard, or freezer, to enable you to whip up a first-class meal, literally from soup to nuts, should the unexpected happen – uninvited company arriving at your door, a sudden earthquake, snowstorm, avalanche. Your motto, remembered since your childhood scouting days, still remains: Be prepared.

You know where to spend and where to save. You always bring back bottles and redeem cents-off coupons. If there is a 'special' the Capricorn will buy it. If it is sold in bulk, you will surely purchase it. You are an incredible bargain hunter and will travel great distances to get the best discounts, then freeze and save the bargains you bought. You go through almost as much freezer paper and aluminium foil as toilet tissue. Your careful methods of food preparation do not always allow for shortcuts, however. Convenience products and TV dinners have always been regarded as something less than substantial. Capricorns are frugal and resourceful. You will closely watch the cashier at the checkout counter as he or she rings up your merchandise, and you will not be shy to request a recheck of the register because 'there is no way those few items could add up to so much'. You are very loyal to neighbourhood vendors even so. You often create goodwill and as a result get just a little bit more service and price breaks than other patrons. You are food savvy, and your local grocers learn fast enough that no one can pull the wool over Capricorn's eyes. You have a collection of helpful shopping hints worthy of a professional home economist. Some food and diet wisdom my practical Capricorn friends have taught me:

- 'Delicious' apples are the sweetest and the best.
- Diet bread is often ordinary bread sliced thinner. Look for calories per ounce.
- Anything that is marked 'dietetic' is immediately twice the price.

You hate to see food wasted, Capricorn. If an item is a day old or not looking too fresh, you will bring it to the attention of the supermarket manager and then request a discount. Tonight's dinner is sure to include the freshest and ripest groceries you bought this afternoon, and the week's menus will be carefully planned around the food on hand in your refrigerator. Of course, you always turn packages over to see the 'consume-by' date before you purchase them. One of these days, some impossible package code like $6 - 7 - 1 - 2 - 1$ will be cracked by a feisty Capricorn.

SOCIAL DINING

Think about your dinner last night Capricorn. You were dining alone and, as always in your singular state, you ate very simply. You have been known to frequent the local delicatessen when the urge for a corned beef sandwich becomes overwhelming. But your choice yesterday was a good old-fashioned cafeteria with steam tables, plenty of hot food, and inexpensive prices.

Now, *social* dining is altogether a horse of another colour. Then you like to dine in fine restaurants. Admit it, Capricorn, there is a part of you that is a social climber, and especially in business you feel it is important to impress your clients with the choice of a superb restaurant, perhaps one in which the maître d' greets you by name. You enjoy transacting business where you might be noticed. Let us not forget, making the proper business deal means money to Capricorn, and money represents security in your life. You are smart enough to keep your alcohol consumption to a minimum because you would never want to lose control. Fortunately, this helps curb the temptation to stray from your diet on these endless 'power' breakfasts, luncheons, dinners.

You do like to keep your life as predictable as possible. You often consult restaurant guides because you like to know what you are in for. When you find a restaurant you like, you will go back to it over and over again, even several times in the same week. You are never entirely comfortable choosing from a menu with no prices. And even at one of the finer dining establishments, you will send back your food if it has not been properly prepared: it has to be perfect.

When you are not closing some important business deal, you hard-driving Capricorns do know how to create romance. You are apt to choose a French bistro where the melodic chords of a violin and harp are heard in the background and the decor, the food and the people are *très* chic. But your personal preference on an evening out with friends might lead you to a hearty dinner at a rustic old inn. You enjoy the country charm of wood panelling, richly coloured upholstery and overstuffed chairs. Underneath it all, you Capricorns are meat-and-potato types. Somehow, it is difficult to imagine you ordering consommé, even the jellied kind. Do you even know what colour it is?

SPECIAL-OCCASION DINING

Normally, you Capricorns are quite reserved and responsible, and that is why special occasions are so troublesome for you – just because they are special. You tend to give yourself licence at these times to do what you wouldn't consider doing at any other, that is, let yourself go. You get surprisingly sentimental at such events as Christmas, your birthday, your mother's birthday, even your cat's birthday. But please beware. These feelings should not be interpreted as signals to digress from your diet. Should your cat's birthday take place during your ten-day diet, it is all right to celebrate, but choose wisely, eat small portions of whatever you wish. Do not worry about offending the host or hostess, and for goodness sake remember: it is only one meal, not an excuse for a three day feast.

Plan your own event if you are in the mood to attend one. You are generally so habitual in your behaviour, that any activity out of the usual is something for you to look forward to, even if the occasion is unrelated to food. If it's a wedding, think of the occasion as time to dance. If it's a picnic, think of it as an opportunity to play a game of football or tennis. Allow yourself to enjoy the pleasure of doing something different, and it will satisfy you just as much as overindulging in goodies.

I know I can depend on you Capricorns to take the necessary precautions to avoid blowing your diet completely when a tempting occasion arises. First of all, you can prepare by cutting down your food intake the day before a festivity, and also on the day following, in order to successfully continue your weight loss programme. You can also cook or bake something in advance to take along to the special occasion. You love to do things like that anyway, and that way you can guarantee all the ingredients in at least one dish are low-calorie. No guilt, no remorse, no cheating, no negative thoughts. Just forgive yourself this one special meal and just pick up your diet wherever you left off.

YOUR HEALTH

As adults, Capricorns are known to have strong, healthy bodies, although as children your constitution is sometimes fragile and weak. Cramps and stomach-aches often kept you home from school in your youth. Sensitive, worrisome Capricorn, your stomach is often the barometer of your emotions. Whenever you are in a stressful situation or undergoing emotional upheaval, your stomach starts to churn. It is a weakness you have learned to camouflage as you have grown older, appearing calm and confident to the rest of the world. However, your cool exterior does not fool your digestive organs. Your constant drive for success and your ambitious, hard-working nature can wreak havoc on your nerves, and there are times you worry so much about your health that friends might have said you are a hypochondriac.

You should never eat when you are upset. Shoving food in your mouth to assuage nervous tension is not what your Capricorn body needs. You need to take a big breath, sit down, and relax. It is especially important that you develop some outside recreation hobby that is simply fun. It will serve to bring a little more balance in your otherwise hard driving life. You know, Cap, you place too much emphasis on your career and station in life.

In medical astrology, Capricorn rules the patella, knees, joints, bones, epidermis, process of the gallbladder, and by reflex action the stomach.

Diseases to which Capricorns are subject but which may or may not manifest themselves in your lifetime:

Allergies	Glaucoma
Arthritis and rheumatism	Hearing disorders
Curvature of the spine	Poor posture
Dental problems	Problems in the joints
Depression	Sciatica
Excess calcium deposits	Skin diseases (rashes,
Excess perspiration	eczema)
Frequent colds	Slipped discs
Gall bladder problems	Sluggish circulation
	Weak knees

Your ruling cell salt is calcium phosphate which helps to build strong bones and teeth. Cell salts are naturally occurring minerals that are normal constituents of the body cells. They are found in trace amounts in foods, because both plants and animals and human beings require these compounds for proper nutrition. And, like vitamins, cell salts get used up.

FOOD RICH IN CALCIUM PHOSPHATE

Almonds	Cucumbers
Asparagus	Egg yolk
Barley	Lean meats
Beans	Plums
Cabbage	Spinach
Celery	Strawberries
	Whole wheat

The Capricorn diet must be high protein, rich in foods that contain high amounts of vitamins A, all the Bs, but especially riboflavin (B-2), C, D, E, calcium, lecithin, and fibre. Lack of these nutrients may cause gall stones, or burning sensation in the upper chest, pain beneath one or both shoulder blades, sharp chest pains, and an inability to catch your breath. Sometimes, you may experience trouble assimilating calcium, so you should be sure to include milk and milk products as often as possible. Additionally, because of your sensitive stomach, it would be wise to avoid very cold or iced drinks. And don't worry so much.

Your Capricorn Reducing Diet has taken all of the above nutritional needs into account to guarantee you your weight will be lost and you will feel better than ever.

CAPRICORN DAILY NUTRITIONAL SUPPLEMENTS

- One general multivitamin with minerals
- One multiple vitamin B-complex (B-100)
- 2,000 mg vitamin C with bioflavinoids
- 200 IU units vitamin E
- 600 – 800 mg OS-cal (calcium carbonate from oyster shells)

REMEMBER, CAPRICORN . . .

This diet is especially prepared to address your sun sign and *should not be interchanged with any other sun sign diet*. It is important that you follow the diet exactly as it appears, for optimum weight loss and assimilation. Before starting your Capricorn diet, carefully read the 'General Diet and Maintenance Guidelines for All Sun Signs' found at the beginning of this book. Remember, drink 8 glasses of water daily.

After you reach your desired weight, turn to the end of the chapter and you will find a long list of the maintenance foods you should incorporate in your diet of programmed Capricorn eating for the rest of your life. Remember, that these are the special foods that your body needs.

Make this a lifetime of eating with the stars.

The Capricorn Ten-Day Reducing Diet

Capricorn, this is a down-to-earth, realistic diet designed for your maximum weight loss and will allow you to gain control over your eating problems. You will find that the Capricorn Ten-Day Reducing Diet will meet the demands of your active lifestyle as well as your nutritional, chemical, and metabolic requirements for good health, putting you back in control of your eating behaviour.

The first three days are supercharged with fruit, an important aid in the digestion and assimilation process. Fruits act as a catalyst, firing up your metabolic system to burn proteins and carbohydrates more efficiently. Days Five through Ten offer many options within the reducing day categories to allow you some freedom in planning your menus. I know I can count on your self-discipline and motivation to follow this precisely.

Your Sun Sign Diet even provides for your cravings for creamy comfort foods. You will find the day of bananas and milk totally satisfying while still allowing you to stay in control of your diet.

To speed up your weight loss even further and additionally suppress your appetite, I would like to suggest the use of dietary fibre sold in the United States under the name of Glucomannan whose UK equivalent should be available from any health food shop. Glucomannan is extracted from the Japanese Konjac root, a tuber known to be exceptionally high in fibre. This root has been cultivated and eaten in Asia for over a thousand years.

Dietary fibre also contributes to substantial decrease in cholesterol and triglyceride levels and aids in low density lyproprotein levels. Dietary fibre increases viscosity and moisture content of food as it is digested. For this reason the food mixes with it to form a smooth, soft mass which moves easily through the intestinal tract. Because digestion is slowed, large swings in blood glucose are avoided and normal blood sugar levels are maintained after a meal. I recommend that you take two capsules three times a day. Watch your appetite cut in half.

Please note the asterisked (*) items which appear after certain foods listed in your menu plan. You will find a detailed explanation of their vitamin and mineral content, and direct information as to why they are essential components of your successful diet regime located in the section marked, 'Capricorn Reducing Diet Notes'.

Follow the diet exactly as designed; do not mix your menus. Eat what is scheduled for that day. (If you do not want something, leave it out, but do not substitute.) This diet is nutritiously balanced so as to allow you to use it for the duration of your entire weight loss. Just repeat the ten menus to see results week after week.

Underneath that cool, disciplined facade of yours, Capricorn, you really are a mere mortal soul like the rest of us. With this in consideration, I have included a binge day for you too. When you begin to feel that you are really going to lose your cool — absolutely blow your top, use your Capricorn Total Binge Day. But remember, no more than four times a month.

This dynamic diet combined with your self-control and discipline, Capricorn, is your key to success.

Good luck, and *go for it*.

DAY ONE – ALL FRUIT DAY*

BREAKFAST

    1 apple or 1 whole grapefruit

LUNCH

    an assorted fresh fruit plate* – up to 3 cups of any
    fruit you wish
    black coffee, tea, or water
    Absolutely nothing else.

MID-AFTERNOON

    1 whole grapefruit

DINNER

    an assorted fresh fruit plate – up to 3 cups of any
    fruit you wish
    black coffee,* tea, or water
    Absolutely nothing else.
    No low-calorie fizzy drinks today*

Remember, drink 8 glasses of water every day.

DAY TWO – ALL BANANA AND MILK DAY*

BREAKFAST

1 banana and 8 oz skimmed milk or buttermilk (put in blender with ice cubes, add sweetener).

LUNCH AND DINNER

4 bananas and 2 more glasses of skimmed milk or buttermilk, spaced throughout the day

(You may freeze peeled bananas in aluminium foil; freeze for at least 4 hours. [May be left in freezer up to 4 days.] They taste like ice cream.)

Remember, drink 8 glasses of water every day.

DAY THREE – FRUIT AND PROTEIN DAY

BREAKFAST AND LUNCH

Choice of:
1 whole fresh pineapple*
4 whole papayas*
4 – 5 cups fresh strawberries*

DINNER

Choose satisfying portions of:*
Baked or broiled chicken, turkey, filet of sole, flounder, lean meat, or veal chop

and

2 sliced tomatoes seasoned with basil and oregano

BEVERAGE

Perrier, café espresso with a twist of lime, tea, Red Zinger*, or a herbal tea of choice

Remember, drink 8 glasses of water every day.

DAY FOUR

BREAKFAST

4 oz cranberry juice or orange juice
¼ cup bran buds or flakes*
1 cup skimmed milk

LUNCH

4 oz sliced chicken, turkey, or cold roast beef
1 bread stick
salad: lettuce, sliced tomato, fresh mushrooms, watercress, and parsley, seasoned with 2 tbs no-oil salad dressing or lemon juice and herbs
iced tea, hot tea, Perrier or fruit juice

SNACK

10–15 pistachio nuts

DINNER

Fish and whole wheat spaghetti*
4 oz glass white wine or champagne (optional)
6 oz any broiled or baked fish in lemon juice, with 1 cup whole wheat pasta mixed with 2 tbsp Mexican salsa*
salad of watercress,* parsley,* lettuce and radishes
café espresso with lemon peel or your choice of beverage

or

Crabmeat and Artichoke Surprise
6 oz fresh or frozen crabmeat (any supermarket)
9 oz box frozen artichokes (Defrost and mix with 8

black olives, ½ cup plain yoghurt, 3 scallions, one
bunch watercress.* Beat in blender and pour over
crabmeat.)
low-calorie jelly – as much as you wish

Remember, drink 8 glasses of water every day.

DAYS FIVE THROUGH TEN

You have a choice of five breakfasts and five lunches. You may vary them, or eat the same one every day. The choice is yours. Each choice is combined to release the highest amount of energy and nutrition for you. You can eliminate but you cannot add or change the combinations given. Do not exceed programmed quantities if you wish to achieve maximum results.

BREAKFAST

Choice of:

1 cup plain yoghurt

or

4 oz skimmed-milk ricotta cheese*

or

4 oz low-fat cottage cheese, sprinkled with 2 tbsp unsalted sunflower seeds, sugar substitute, and cinnamon may be added if desired.
coffee with a little milk, tea, or herbal tea

or

Strawberry or Papaya Smash Drink*

Blend 1 cup fresh strawberries or ⅔ cup unsugared frozen strawberries, or one whole papaya with a packet of vanilla flavoured skimmed milk. Beat with 2 ice cubes until frothy.
black coffee, tea, or herbal tea

or

Blackberries

1½ cups fresh blackberries* or 1 package unsweetened frozen blackberries
black coffee, tea, or herbal tea (Sugar substitute allowed, but absolutely no milk products with this breakfast).

or

Scrambled Egg, Cheese and Salsa

Scramble one egg in nonstick pan with 2 oz skimmed-milk ricotta cheese and 2 tbsp Mexican salsa. Delicious and nutritious.
coffee with milk

or

Toast and Juice (once per week)

1 slice of toasted wholemeal bread with 1 tsp cream cheese and diet jam
4 oz unsweetened grapefruit juice or ½ grapefruit

LUNCH

Choice of:

Apple Spinach Cheese Peanut Salad

Raw spinach leaves with 1 sliced apple, 3 oz low-fat cottage cheese, 10 unsalted peanuts (or 5 pecans), and 1 tbsp raisins
café au lait, espresso, or iced tea

or

Pasta Delight with Apple* *(once per week)*

one whole apple (Eat ten minutes before pasta so that enzymes from apple will act to digest pasta more efficiently).

Pasta

1 cup durum wheat or whole wheat pasta cooked with garlic, pepper, oregano, herbs, and pimentos. Season with 1 tsp diet margarine
café espresso, black coffee with lemon peel, or Perrier with a twist of lime

or

Fresh Fruit Plate

Consisting of ½ cantaloup melon or ½ grapefruit, ½ orange, ½ pear, ¼ pineapple, ½ apple, and 15 grapes. If eating at restaurant, you may order up to 2 cups absolutely fresh fruit salad.
black coffee, iced tea, hot tea, or herbal tea (absolutely no milk may be consumed with this meal).

or

Baked Potato Feast*

1 very large baked potato served with ¼ cup plain yoghurt and seasoned with dill, chives, scallions, garlic and thyme, served on a bed of lettuce and spinach leaves.
Perrier with a twist of lime, or hot tea

or

2 Hard Boiled Eggs Salad

Slice 2 hard boiled eggs and serve with 1 whole sliced tomato seasoned with basil and oregano.

1 cup salad consisting of watercress, spinach, and parsley seasoned with lemon juice and garlic pepper.

Perrier with a twist of lime

DINNER

1 cup low-calorie soup (herb, beef, tomato, chicken)

and

a large salad every day consisting of the following:

Broccoli	Escarole
Cauliflower	Green pepper
Celery	Lettuce
Chinese cabbage	Mushrooms
Cucumber	Spinach
Endive	String beans
	Watercress

Use 2 – 3 tbsp no-oil salad dressing, or lemon juice and garlic powder.

Choice of 4 – 6 oz baked, broiled, or steamed (no butter, just lemon juice):

Herring (3½ oz)	Flounder
Tinned salmon (4 oz)	Halibut
Chicken	Lobster (1 – 1½ lb)
Chicken livers	Pacific sardines (3½ oz)
Codfish	Red Snapper
Crabmeat	Salmon
Filet of sole	Shrimp

and

Choice of 1 cup: cooked cauliflower, broccoli, spinach, asparagus, or 1 whole fresh artichoke, served with warm lemon juice and garlic pepper and dill topped with 1 tbs Parmesan cheese.
For dessert: unlimited amounts of low-calorie jelly with 2 tbsp low-calorie instant whip

or

1 lemon sorbet*
decaffeinated coffee, espresso coffee with a twist of lime, tea, rose hip herbal tea, or chamomile, Perrier
That's it. Repeat day one to continue diet.

Remember, drink 8 glasses of water every day.

NOTES TO CAPRICORN TEN-DAY REDUCING DIET

Day One

- Fresh fruit is fortified with powerful enzymes which act to digest food, speed up your metabolism, and to rid the body of accumulated toxins. As the fruit begins to cleanse your system, you will notice a feeling of elevation, lightness, energy. The diuretic nature of many of the fruits will result in increased urination today.
- No milk allowed today. If you choose to have coffee for your beverage, it is absolutely imperative that you do not consume even the smallest bit of milk. Milk products will stop the enzyme action of the fruit and you will prevent a good weight loss.
- No fizzy drinks today. The chemicals, additives, and preservatives in carbonated drinks similarly inhibit the enzyme action of the fruits.

Day Two

I am sure that you are pleased with your weight loss this morning, Capricorn, and you will find the same results with today's menu.

- The calcium-rich skimmed milk or buttermilk combined with a banana (supplying 370 mg of potassium, 33 mg of magnesium, vitamin C and B-6) fills your vitamin requirements. In addition, the above vitamin combination is especially calming to the nerves, a usual Capricorn complaint. You may space your lunch and dinner any way you wish. You will hardly even feel like you are dieting.

Day Three

The fruit and protein combination has been designed for ultimate weight loss but high energy output.

- Once again, your breakfast and lunch is packed with live enzyme fruit. You have a choice of either pineapple, papaya, or grapefruit. Pineapple is rich in chlorine, has an invigorating effect upon an overworked liver, has natural diuretic properties, and it is one of the highest enzyme fruits. Papaya, rich in vitamins C, B, and A, and the enzyme digestive juice 'papain' has a soothing effect on the stomach and intestinal tract. Fresh strawberries are vitamin C-rich and another good choice for you. Do not mix your fruits. Whichever fruit you choose, you must have it at both breakfast and lunch.
- I have not listed a specific amount of protein for your dinner menu; by now, your body is ready to tell you when you have had enough. If you choose to have coffee for a beverage, it must not contain any milk.

- Red Zinger tea is available from most UK health food shops, and is made by Celestial Seasonings Ltd.

Day Four

- Constipation and Capricorn seem to be synonymous. Bran Buds or flakes for breakfast today.
- Lunch and dinner are high riboflavin menus. Remember riboflavin functions as part of a group of enzymes that are involved in the breakdown and utilization of carbohydrates, proteins and fats.
- Today you have a choice of two dinners. Many of you are looking for spaghetti at this point in your diet regime. However, make sure that you use durum wheat spaghetti.
- Mexican salsa is made of chili peppers which are extremely rich in vitamin A and C. They are good for the digestive and circulatory system.

MEXICAN SALSA

1 6 oz/175 g tomato
½ medium onion
6 sprigs fresh coriander
3 chilli peppers
½ tsp salt
3 fl oz/8 cl cold water

Chop tomato, onion, coriander and peppers finely. Do not skin tomato or seed the peppers. Mix them together in a bowl and add the salt and water.

- It is important that you have your salad of watercress and parsley. Both vegetables are rich in calcium and vitamin C and substitute your need for milk.

Days Five through Ten

I can always count on my Capricorn friends for staying well within the guidelines and rules of any diet and for this reason give you the option to make your choices from your programmed meals.

All the breakfasts and lunches have been designed for optimum weight loss, while meeting all your Capricorn nutritional requirements. If you do not want to eat everything programmed for a particular meal, leave it out. Make no substitutions.

You will experience a wonderful feeling of well-being as the pounds just melt off.

Some Food Facts You Will Want to Know for Reducing Days Five through Ten

- Potatoes are very rich in potassium. Their satiating power will keep the hunger pangs away.
- Asparagus is an excellent diuretic food, containing vitamin B-1 (thiamin). It also contains the enzyme asparagine which helps to break up accumulated fats in the cells.
- Sunflower seeds are rich in B-6, potassium, magnesium, calcium, fibre, and lecithin. Especially good for the brain and nerve tissues.
- Hard boiled eggs have long satiety value, take almost as much caloric energy to digest as the egg yields, and contains 6 grams of protein. A good source of vitamins A, B-2, D, E, folic acid, phosphorus, and iron.
- Just 3½ oz broccoli, rich in vitamin A and all the Bs, has 267 mg of potassium and 1.5 mg of fibre.
- 3½ oz cottage cheese is rich in riboflavin as well as other B vitamins and calcium.
- Chicken is a good source of vitamins B-2, B-3, B-6, B-12, and folic acid.
- 3½ oz of watercress has 606 mg of potassium,

50 mg of folic acid, and is chock full of vitamins A, B-2, C, as well as fibre.

- Herring alots 20 grams of protein per serving and is rich in vitamin B-2, B-3, B-6, B-12, and D, phosphorus, calcium, and potassium.
- Sardines supply you with vitamin B-2, B-3, B-12, D, iron, magnesium, potassium, and 525 mg of calcium (that's twice the amount in an 8 oz glass of milk).
- 3½ oz cooked lobster meat has 128 grams of protein and only 95 calories.

LEMON SORBET

1 pint of water
6 oz granulated sugar
3 lemons, rind and juice of
Put the rind in a saucepan with the sugar and water. Dissolve completely over a low heat, then boil rapidly for 5–6 minutes. Set aside, cool, add the lemon juice, mix and strain. Chill and freeze.

(This will give 10 portions at 66 calories per portion or 20 half-portions at 33 calories.)

CAPRICORN TOTAL BINGE DAY

Capricorn, there are times when you need to let go. I have given you that option with a binge day. Now remember, Capricorn, you have a tendency to go overboard, so be careful.

Before You Binge

1. Drink water.
2. Drink water.
3. Drink water.
4. Rest.
5. Brush your teeth and rinse with your favourite mouthwash.
6. Chew sugarless gum for 20 minutes.

You may find that the desire to binge has passed. However, if you are still suffering from intense food frustration, follow these basic binge rules:

Rule Number One

Under no circumstances should you ever binge before completing Day Six of your reducing diet. This will ensure a maximum weight loss with a minimum of food frustration.

Rule Number Two

If, for example, you binge on the sixth day of your diet, resume your diet the following day (Day Seven) with the menu for Day Six. If you binge for just one meal, such as lunch on Day Six, resume your reducing diet with dinner on Day Six of your reducing diet.

Rule Number Three

Bingeing is for when you get that creepy, anxious feeling, when you feel like pulling out your hair – strand by strand – and you cannot endure dieting for even one more moment. Before you climb the walls, give yourself a binge day. It's hoped that this will not be necessary more than four times a month.

Rule Number Four

After you have lost your first 10 pounds, you may vary your binge day with the binge day of the sun sign opposite yours, which is Cancer (see below). Remember, an occasional binge day – when necessary – will still allow you to lose weight (without guilt).

CAPRICORN BINGE DAY MENU

BREAKFAST

½ cantaloup melon or ½ orange or 4 oz orange juice and 1 wholemeal roll with 1 tablespoon peanut butter and diet jam and café au lait (2 oz regular milk)

or

½ cantaloup melon or ½ orange or 4 oz orange juice and 1 frozen toaster waffle with 1 tbsp golden syrup and 1 tbsp Bird's Dream Topping and café au lait (2 oz regular milk)

LUNCH

1 frankfurter with sauerkraut and mustard on roll and ½ cup vanilla, chocolate, strawberry, and coffee ice cream
fruit juice

or

1 serving Black Forest Gateau with 1 cup fresh or frozen strawberries and café au lait (2 oz regular milk)

or

1 slice pizza with mushrooms with ½ cup tofu mixed with puréed fruit and fruit juice

DINNER

1 light beer or 4 oz white wine or sangria
1 6 oz hamburger or ½ barbecued chicken and 10 fried chipped potatoes
large tossed salad with 2 tbsp salad dressing of your choice

SNACK

Low-fat/skimmed-milk flavoured drink with 1 tsp whipped cream topping

CANCER BINGE DAY MENU

BREAKFAST

½ Cantaloup melon or 4 oz orange juice
1 bran or wholemeal roll with diet margarine and diet jam
1 frothy low-fat chocolate drink

or

4 oz orange juice
¼ cup granola cereal with skimmed milk and 1 tsp raisins

or

The Cancer Cheater Drink

1 ripe papaya or ½ fresh pineapple cut in chunks, juice of 1 orange. 1 big strawberry, and 1 ice cube. Beat in blender . . . sinful and delicious
½ toasted roll with diet margarine
coffee

LUNCH

1 all-beef frankfurter (only one bun) loaded with sauerkraut and mustard
½ cup vanilla ice cream
Perrier

or

1 slice of pizza
1 scoop vanilla, chocolate, strawberry, or coffee ice cream
fruit juice

DINNER

1 cup spaghetti with 3 oz flaked tuna and 2 tbsp caviar seasoned with basil, oregano, grated Parmesan cheese, with a scant tablespoon oil and garlic pepper
20 frozen grapes for dessert (place in freezer 6 hours earlier)

or

Any broiled or baked fish with salad
large house salad with 1 tbsp dressing and 2 pieces
garlic bread

Maintaining Your Ideal Weight

CAPRICORN MAINTENANCE FOODS FOR OPTIMUM HEALTH

You Are What You Eat

When you have achieved your desired weight goal you should follow a maintenance diet rich in the specific nutrients that you, Capricorn, need each and every day.

CALCIUM

There is more calcium in the body than any other mineral, and almost all of the body's calcium is found in the bones and teeth. Because 20 per cent of an adult's bone calcium has to be replaced every year (due to new bone cell formation, and because old cells break down), it is vital that you replenish your supply of calcium. Capricorn rules over the bones in your body and Capricorns tend to have back problems more than any other sun sign. The proper amount of calcium will help prevent fragile and brittle bones, arthritis, atherosclerosis, leg cramps, acne, and nail problems.

Calcium aids your nervous system, alleviates insomnia, and prevents rickets. In addition, calcium assists the blood clotting process and helps regulate the balance of alkali to acid in the blood. When calcium is combined with magnesium the ratio should be 2:1, twice as much calcium as magnesium. For adults, 800 – 1,200 mg of calcium is the RDA.

VITAMIN A

You need vitamin A, Capricorn, to help maintain clear, bright healthy eyes and skin. In fact, vitamin A plays a significant part in protecting your skin from premature aging as well as acne. It is absolutely essential for protein metabolism in the liver where approximately 85 per cent of the body's vitamin A is stored. Vitamins A and E play an important part in protecting your lung tissue. However, taking supplementary vitamin A pills can be toxic, and unless advised by your physician should be avoided. Vitamin A should be derived from the following food sources.

FOODS RICH IN VITAMIN A

(Think of yellow and orange-coloured fruits and vegetables)

Bananas
Beets
Broccoli
Broiled liver
Cantaloup melon
Carrots
Chicken liver
Egg yolk

Mangos
Oranges
Parsley
Peaches
Potatoes
Red chili peppers
Salmon
Squash
Yams

THE B VITAMIN GROUP

The more you worry, the more depressed you become and the more you need a healthy supply of foods rich in vitamin B. I have yet to meet a group of greater 'worriers' than Capricorns. The B-complex group maintains muscle tone in the gastrointestinal tract, and aids in the general functioning of the nervous system. A diet supplying sufficient B vitamins makes for a healthy gallbladder.

One very important member of the B-complex group for the Capricorn constitution is vitamin B-2, or riboflavin.

VITAMIN B-2 (RIBOFLAVIN)

Riboflavin functions as part of a group of enzymes that are involved in the breakdown and utilization of carbohydrates, fats, and protein, and regulates the delicate sodium-potassium balance in the body. Most recently, studies have linked a deficiency of riboflavin with anaemia and hypoglycaemia (low blood sugar). Stomach cramps, ear infections and cracks at the corners of your mouth are indications that your riboflavin intake may be too low.

Capricorn, you require more riboflavin foods in your diet than any other sun sign because you do have a proclivity towards problems involving the eyes, such as conjunctivitis, glaucoma, night blindness, cataracts, impaired vision, and eye fatigue. You will note that your Capricorn Reducing Diet is chock full of riboflavin foods.

In combination with vitamin A, riboflavin maintains the health of the mucous membranes throughout the body and especially protects the skin. Oily skin, itching, scaling of the scalp, dermatitis, and even acne should have you questioning your riboflavin intake.

FOODS RICH IN RIBOFLAVIN

All dairy products	Milk
Apples	Papaya
Beef	Parsley
Broccoli	Peanuts
Celery	Salmon
Cottage cheese	Soya bean products
Dark-green leafy vegetables	Spinach
Dried apricots	Strawberries
Eggs	Tomatoes
Lecithin granules	Veal
Liver	Watercress
Mangos	Yoghurt

VITAMIN C

Vitamin C is one of the vitamins the body cannot manufacture for itself, or store from day to day. This is true for every sign, but for you, Capricorn, it has particular importance.

Vitamin C aids in all forms of gum disease, such as bleeding gums, soft and receding gums, phyorrhea, and tooth cavities – all common Capricorn complaints. (Most Capricorns spend a good deal of time and money at the periodontist.) Vitamin C has been proven to lessen most allergy, hay fever and asthma problems, and, of course, your usual yearly bout of bacterial and/or viral upper-respiratory infections.

This marvellous vitamin also helps to heal wounds and bone fractures, and it decreases swelling in painful joints. It also helps the body to form collagen, when, if retained in insufficient supply, it may cause the cells in your bones to lose their supportive strength. Because Capricorns are prone to back and knee problems, you should be certain that you always have an adequate supply of vitamin C, as included in your Capricorn Reducing Diet.

FOODS RICH IN VITAMIN C

Almonds	Grapefruit
Apples	Green peppers
Asparagus	Lemons
Bananas	Oranges
Beets	Orange juice
Broccoli	Parsley
Brussel sprouts	Pineapple
Cantaloup melon	Skimmed milk
Carrots	Strawberries
Celery	Tomatoes
Currants	Watercress

VITAMIN D

Without adequate vitamin D, the body could not properly assimilate calcium. The result would be soft bones. Your back and spine are sensitive areas for all Capricorns and so you must be sure to have an adequate intake of vitamin D.

Vitamin D improves absorption and utilization of the calcium and phosphorus required for bone formation. It also helps regulate the nervous system and your heart's rhythmic action. In addition, recent research indicates that vitamin D may play an important role in alleviating arthritic pain, so often a Capricorn complaint.

FOODS RICH IN VITAMIN D

Bass	Oysters
Butter	Salmon
Cheese	Sardines
Herring	Shrimp
Liver	Sunflower seeds
Mackerel	Tuna
Milk	Watercress
Mushrooms	Yoghurt

BIOFLAVINOIDS

Bioflavinoids act with vitamin C to prevent cholesterol build up, which can cause clotting of the arteries, veins, and capillaries. Bioflavinoids act with vitamin C to maintain 'clean blood'. Because of anticlotting effect, bioflavinoids can also be quite effective in preventing varicose veins.

FOODS RICH IN BIOFLAVINOIDS

Apples
Apricots
Blackberries
Blackcurrants
Buckwheat
Cherries
Grapes
Grapefruit
Green Pepper
Lemons
Oranges
Parsley

Peanut butter
Prunes
Spinach
Salmon
Sardines
Shrimp
Spinach
Sunflower seeds
Sweet potato
Turkey
Wheat germ

VITAMIN E

Vitamin E's most important function is to serve as an antioxidant and antiaging vitamin. It prevents red blood cells from combining with toxic peroxide and instead promotes their combining with oxygen. Vitamin E also helps to dissolve blood clots and dilates the blood vessels so that oxygen-rich blood is freely carried to all parts of the body.

Many specific health problems, Capricorn, result from impaired circulation – varicose veins, for example. Because of vitamin E's positive effect on circulation, it both prevents and relieves varicose veins.

FOODS RICH IN VITAMIN E

Apples
Asparagus
Avocados
Broccoli

Chicken
Eggs
Halibut
Liver

Cabbage	Milk
Carrots	Mushrooms
Cheese	Parsley

LECITHIN

Lecithin is an emulsifying agent: it breaks down large fat globules into microscopic bits, which helps prevent cholesterol plaque from forming on the walls of your arteries. Lecithin, one of the ingredients in bile, acts to break down fats aiding the function of the gallbladder. Capricorns do have a sensitivity to gallbladder problems and for this reason it is a good idea to have adequate lecithin in your diet.

FOODS RICH IN LECITHIN

Avocado	Rice
Barley	Sesame seeds
Beef	Sunflower seeds
Chicken	Tuna
Liver	Turkey
Milk	Veal

SAMPLE MAINTENANCE MENU

When you reach your desired goal, please follow the maintenance eating hints found in the 'General Diet and Maintenance Guidelines for All Sun Signs' at the beginning of this book for proper calculations of caloric intake.

I'm including a sample maintenance menu based on your Sun Sign for optimal Capricorn maintenance. Try to choose many of the foods you eat from your Capricorn Maintenance Food list.

SAMPLE CAPRICORN MAINTENANCE MENU 2,000 CALORIES PER DAY

BREAKFAST	CALORIES
2 in wedge honeydew melon	50
2 egg omelette with 1 oz swiss cheese made with 1 tbsp diet butter	300
1 toasted wholemeal roll	145
Coffee or tea	0
	495

LUNCH	
4 oz dry white wine (optional)	75
½ avocado stuffed with ½ cup crabmeat and endive on a bed of lettuce	298
1 dinner roll with 1 tsp butter	130
coffee, tea, or fruit juice	0
	503

MID-AFTERNOON SNACK	
1 cup fresh strawberries	45

DINNER

4 oz dry red wine (optional)	75
5 – 6 oz roast beef	575
1 cup braised celery and mushrooms	50
1 baked potato with 1 tbsp sour cream and chives	120
green leafy salad with alfalfa sprouts, watercress, parsley, seasoned with lemon juice, garlic, and dill	100
	820

SNACK

1 cup any flavour ice milk	160

TOTAL DAILY CALORIES

2023

Remember, drink 8 glasses of water every day.

Restaurant Eating the Capricorn Way

Perhaps you have seen the following dishes on restaurant menus. Maybe you have ordered them, and maybe not. Included here are dishes chosen to appeal specifically to the Capricorn palate. Note that all of the recommended dishes contain the nutrients especially important for you and which are included in your Capricorn maintenance food lists. All the foods listed are prepared lightly and are good restaurant choices for low calorie eating. Note the high level of calcium foods and vitamin D, especially found in the salmon and sweetbreads. Note the incorporation of pasta and cheese dishes, especially akin to Capricorn. In all cases, one appetizer plus one entrée equals approximately 500–600 calories.

FRENCH RESTAURANT

APPETIZERS

Eggplant with caviar
Salad of crabmeat and lemon

ENTRÉE

Seafood baked in a light wine sauce
Loin of lamb with fresh mint
Braised sweetbreads with mushrooms
Chicken in wine sauce

ITALIAN RESTAURANT

APPETIZERS

Thinly sliced beef with herb sauce
Roasted fresh peppers and anchovies

ENTRÉES

Fettucini and ricotta cheese with sage
Veal in a green basil sauce

Striped bass in wine, capers and anchovies
Veal cutlet stuffed with ricotta cheese and spinach

CHINESE RESTAURANT

APPETIZERS

Wonton Soup
Chicken Egg Drop Soup

ENTRÉES

Diced chicken with broccoli
Sliced beef with watercress and snow peas
Moo Shu pork with 1 cup white rice
Baby shrimp with steamed water chestnuts in garlic sauce

AMERICAN RESTAURANT

APPETIZERS

Fresh fruit cup
Jumbo shrimps or clams on the half shell

ENTRÉES

Broiled chicken and ribs
Hamburger every way under the Sun
Shrimp and salad bar
Prime ribs au jus

Bibliography

Adams, Catherine. *Nutritive Value of American Foods*. Pamphlet prepared by Agricultural Research Service, US Department of Agriculture, Washington, DC, 1975.

Adams, Rex. *Miracle Medicine Foods*. West Nyack, NY Parker, 1977.

Adams, Ruth. *The Complete Home Guide to All the Vitamins*. New York: Larchmont Books, 1972.

Anderson, Jefferson. *Sun Signs, Moon Signs*. New York: Dell Publishing Co., 1978.

Arroyo, Stephen. *Astrology, Psychology and the Four Elements*. Vancouver, WA: CRCS, 1975.

Bartlett, John. *Bartlett's Familiar Quotations*. 13th ed. Boston: Little, Brown and Company, 1955.

Beilier, Henry G. *Food Is Your Best Medicine*. New York: Random House, 1965.

Bircher-Brenner, M. *Eating Your Way to Health*, New York: Penguin Books, 1973.

Bragg, Paul C. *The Miracle of Fasting*. Burbank, CA: Health Science, 1969.

Brewster, Letitia, and Michael F. Jacobson. *The Changing American Diet*. Pamphlet prepared by Center for Science in the Public Interest. Washington, DC, 1978.

Bricklin, Mark. *The Practical Encyclopedia of Natural Healing*, Emmaus, PA, Rodale Press, 1976.

Bruch, Hilde. *Eating Disorders*. New York: Basic Books, 1973.

Buscaglia, Leo. *Living, Loving, and Learning*. New York: Ballantine Books, 1982.

——. *Loving Each Other*. Thorofare, NJ: Slack, 1984.

——. *Love*. New York: Fawcett Publications, 1972.

Carrington, Hereward. *Fasting for Health and Long Life*. Mokelumne Hill, CA: Health Research, 1953.

Carter, C.E.O. *An Encyclopedia of Psychological Astrology*. London: Theosophical Society, 1963.

Clark, Linda. *Know Your Nutrition*. New Canaan, CT: Keats, 1973.

——. *Rejuvenation*. Old Greenwich, CT: Devin-Adair, 1979.

Corbin, Cheryl. *Nutrition*. New York: Holt, Rinehart and Winston, 1980.

Cornell, Howard Leslie. *Encyclopedia of Medical Astrology*: 3rd ed. New York: Llewellyn and Samuel Weiser, 1972.

Cunningham, Donna. *An Astrological Guide to Self-Awareness*. Vancouver, WA: CRCS, 1978.

Davidson, William M. *Davidson's Medical Astrology*: Monroe, NY: Astrological Bureau, 1979.

Davison, Ronald. *Mundane Astrology*. New York: National Astrological Society, 1975.

DeRosis, Helen A. *Women and Anxiety*. New York: Delacorte Press, 1979.

Dietary Goals for the US. 2nd ed. US Senate, Select Committee on Nutrition and Human Needs. Washington DC: Government Printing Office, 1978.

Dobon, Joel, C. *The Astrologica¹ Secrets of the Hebrew Sages*. New York: Inner Traditions International, Ltd, 1983.

Duff, Howard M. *Astrological Types*. ——, ——: Duff, 1948.

Duz, M. *A Practical Treatise of Astral Medicine and Therapeutics*. London: W. Foulsham, 1966.

Ebertin, ——. *Psychological Interpretation of the Chart*. New York: National Astrological Society, 1973.

Ehret, Arnold, *Mucusless Diet Healing System*. New York: Benedict Lust, 1976.

Epstein, Alan. *Psychodynamics of Injunctions*. York Beach, ME: Samuel Weiser, 1984.

Evans, Jane A. *Twelve Doors to the Soul: Astrology of the Inner Self*. London: Theosophical Society, 1979.

Fredericks, Carlton. *High-Fiber Way to Total Health*. New York: Pocket Books, 1976.

Garten, M.O. *The Natural and Drugless Way for Better Health*. New York: Arc Books, 1969.

Gauquelin, Michael. *How Cosmic and Atmospheric Energies Influence Your Health*. New York: Aurora, 1971.

Geddes, Sheila. *Astrology and Health*. Wellingborough, Northamptonshire, England: Aquarian, 1981.

George, Llewellyn. *A to Z Horoscope and Delineator*. 29th ed. St Paul, MN: Llewellyn, 1973.

Gerras, Charles (ed). *The Encyclopedia of Common Diseases*. Emmaus, PA: Rodale Press, 1976.

Goodman, Linda. *Sun Signs*. New York: Taplinger Publishing Co., 1968.

Gray, Henry. *Gray's Anatomy*. New York: Bounty Books, 1977.

Hand, Robert. *Horoscope Symbols*. Gloucester, MA: Para Research, 1981.

——. *Planets in Transit: Life Cycles for Living*. Gloucester, MA: Para Research, 1976.

——. *Planets in Youth*. Rockport, MA: Para Research, 1977.

Jacobson, Roger. *Calculation of the True Nodes*. New York: National Astrological Society, 1972.

Johnson, Robert A. *We: Understanding the Psychology of Romantic Love*. San Francisco: Harper and Row, 1983.

Keane, Jerryl L. *Practical Astrology: How to Make It Work For You*. West Nyack, NY: Parker, 1967.

Kundalini Research Institute. *Foods for Health and Healing*. Berkeley/ Pomona, CA: Spiritual Community/KRI, 1983.

Landscheidt, ——. *Structures of Prime Numbers and Distances Between Planets*. New York: National Astrological Society, 1973.

Lappé, Frances Moore. *Diet for a Small Planet*. New York: Ballantine Books, 1974.

Lundsted, Betty. *Transits: The Time of Your Life*. York Beach, ME: Samuel Weiser, 1980.

Marks, Tracy. *How to Handle Your T-Square*. Arlington, MA: Sagittarius Rising, 1979.

Marsh, Edward E. *How to be Healthy with Natural Foods*. New York: Gramercy, n.d.

Marshall, Mel. *Real Living with Real Foods*. New York: Fawcett Publications, 1974.

Martine. *Sexual Astrology*. New York: Dell Publishing Co., 1976.

Meyer, Michael R. *A Handbook for the Humanistic Astrologer*. Garden City, NY: Anchor Books, 1974.

Michaels, Marjorie. *Stay Healthy With Wine*. New York: New American Library, 1981.

Newman, Laura. *Make Your Juicer Your Drugstore*. Simi Valley, CA: Benedict Lust, 1972.

Pearson, Durk, and Sandy Shaw. *The Life Extension Companion*. New York: Warner Books, 1983.

Pennington, Jean A.T., and Helen Nichols Church. *Food Values of Portions Commonly Used*. 14th ed. New York: Harper and Row, 1985.

Raphael. *Raphael's Medical Astrology*. Ontario, Canada: Provoker, 1978.

Raman, ——. *The Spiritual Value of Astrology*. New York: National Astrological Society, 1972.

Recommended Dietary Allowances. Washington, DC: National Academy of Sciences, 1979.

Reuben, David. *Everything You Always Wanted to Know About Nutrition*. New York: Avon Books, 1972.

Rosenblum, Bernard. *The Astrologer's Guide to Counseling*. Reno, NV: CRCS, 1983.

Rudhyar, Danr. *The Sun Is Also a Star*. New York: E.P. Dutton, 1975.

Sakokian, Frances, and Louis S. Acker. *The Astrologer's Handbook*. New York: Harper and Row, 1973.

Scott, Cyril. *Cider Vinegar*. Wellingborough, Northamptonshire, England: Aquarian 1968.

Schull, Martin. *Celestial Harmony*. York Beach. ME: Samuel Weiser, 1980.

Shelton, Herbert M. *Fasting Can Save Your Life*. San Antonio, TX: Natural Hygiene Press, 1981.

——. *Food Combining Made Easy*. San Antonio, TX: Dr Shelton's Health School, 1951.

——. *Superior Nutrition*. San Antonio, TX: Dr Shelton's Health School, 1951.

Simonson, Maria, and Joan Rattner Heilman. *The Complete University Medical Diet*. New York: Warner Books, 1983.

Starck, Marcia. *Astrology Key to Holistic Health*. Birmingham, MI: Seek It Publications, 1982.

Sutton, Nancy. *Adventures in Cooking with Health Foods*. New York: Pyramid Press, 1972.

Tarnower, Herman. *The Complete Scarsdale Medical Diet*. New York: Rawson Wade, 1978.

Townley, John. *Planets in Love: Exploring Your Sexual Needs*. Gloucester, MA: Para Research, 1978.

Verrett, Jacqueline, and Jean Carper. *Eating May Be Hazardous to Your Health*. New York: Simon and Schuster, 1974.

Viscott, David. *How to Live With Another Person*. New York: Pocket Books, 1974.

Wangemann, Edith. *The Birthplace Houses*. New York: National Astrological Society, 1972.

Wanson, George. *Nutrition and Your Mind*. New York: Harper and Row, 1972.

Wassmer, Arthur C. *Making Contact*. New York: Fawcett Publications, 1978.

Weingarten, Henry. *The Study of Astrology*. New York: ASI, 1977.

Weiss, Clara A. *Astrological Keys to Self-Actualization and Self-Realization*. New York: Weiser, 1980.

Wentzler, Rich. *The Vitamin Book*. New York: Gramercy Publishing Co., 1978.

Zerof, Herbert G. *Finding Intimacy*. New York: Random House, 1978.

Zolar. *It's All in the Stars*. New York: Fawcett, 1962.